MOSCOW

I0140120

book & lyrics by
Nick Salamone
music by
Maury R McIntyre

BROADWAY PLAY PUBLISHING INC
New York
www.broadwayplaypublishing.com
info@broadwayplaypublishing.com

MOSCOW

Cover image by Jo Anna Perrin

First printing: July 2011. This printing: June 2016
I S B N: 978-0-88145-460-4

Book design: Marie Donovan
Typographic controls & page make-up: Adobe InDesign
Typeface: Palatino

MOSCOW was originally produced by Jon Lawrence
Rivera for Playwrights' Arena at the Lee Strasberg
Theater in Los Angeles in February 1998 with the
following cast:

JON .... Sean Smith
MATT .... Joshua Wolf Coleman
LUKE .... Nic Arnzen

Director .... Jessica Kubzansky
Set & costume design .... John Binkley
Lighting design .... Patrick Welborn
Musical director/pianist .... Chris Lavely
Violinist .... Alma Cielo
Choreographer .... Kitty McNamee

MOSCOW then played at the 1998 Edinburgh
International Fringe Festival with the following cast:

JON .... Clay Storseth
MATT .... Joshua Wolf Coleman
LUKE .... Nic Arnzen

MOSCOW was subsequenly produced by Jon
Lawrence Rivera for Playwrights' Arena and Ginger
Perkins for Frantic Redhead Productions at The French
Institute.

MOSCOW premiered in New York City at the 2002
Chekhov Now Festival at the Connelly Theater with
the following cast:

JON .... Clay Storseth
MATT ....Alan Mingo, Jr
LUKE .... Nic Arnzen

Director... Jessica Kubzansky
Set design .... John Binkley
Costume design .... Jana Rosenblatt
Lighting design ....Jeremy Pivnick
Musical director/pianist.................................... Chris Lavely
Violinist ....Alma Cielo
Flautist.. Tessa Alburn
Choreographer ....Kitty McNamee

The original New York cast recording of MOSCOW,
produced by Lawrence du Buisson, is available on C D.

CHARACTERS & SETTING

<small>LUKE</small>
<small>JON</small>
<small>MATT</small>

an abandoned theater

(The stage is set with only an A-frame ladder or two in usable open position, ropes that hang in disarray from the lighting grid above, bits of fabric from the torn curtains of the stage that might be used by the three men to suggest costumes when they perform in the play within the play, an old trunk, a small foot stool, maybe a torn cyclorama upstage. All to suggest a theater long ago fallen into disuse.)

(Three men are engaged in a game of "sockball" as the audience enters the theater. The men are completely oblivious to the audience of course as they are completely alone in this space and have been for an indeterminate amount of time. LUKE, *the youngest, a southern boy of about twenty is clearly the superior player. Pitching is his specialty and the other men, particularly* JON, *the eldest, a caustic New Yorker of about forty, often strike out. The men use a broken janitor's broom handle as a bat, balled up athletic socks as a ball, and an old theatre seat cushion as a base. The third man,* MATT, *is a black midwesterner of about thirty who, unlike* JON, *is able to find real pleasure in the game. The game continues as the house lights dim.* JON *strikes out, saying:)*

JON: Thank God that's over. It's time.

(As the following dialogue continues, JON *immediately begins to set up for the play within the play. He moves the trunk and footstool assiduously into place to denote various furniture elements.* MATT *helps him, bringing three large swatches of material that have been ripped from the torn hanging curtains which will serve as suggestions of costume.* JON *puts the broken broom handle carefully on the stage*

*floor to denote a window on the fourth wall out of which
they will look and to which they will refer when playing the
upcoming scene from the play within the play.)*

LUKE: You just can't stand to get your ass whupped.

JON: I hardly call lurching around the stage being
chased by a pair of athletic socks in the hands of some
maniacal adolescent cracker getting my ass whupped.

MATT: Give me that broom handle. It's the only one
we've got.

JON: Okay. Are we ready?

LUKE: Right now?

JON: Of course now. The opening. Do you remember
your cue?

LUKE: What cue?

JON: Don't you what cue me.

MATT: I'll prompt him.

JON: Alright, Matt. Would you mind?

MATT: Not at all.

*(The three have taken their curtain remnants and at a signal
from JON ceremoniously and with great flourish shake
their "costumes" open and don them. JON uses his swatch
as a shawl. MATT uses his as a scarf. LUKE uses his as
skirt. LUKE is clearly disrespectful of this ritual even as he
performs it.)*

(And lights up.)

*(The lights shift, growing much warmer. JON will sing as
OLGA, MATT as MASHA, LUKE as IRINA as they rehearse
Chekhov's* Three Sisters*)*

Chekhov's Opening

JON/OLGA:
Father died just a year ago today
Your name day, Irina
The Fifth of May

LUKE: What's a name day again?

JON: It's the feast day of the saint she was named after.

LUKE: Saint Irina? I never heard of Saint Irina. Must be a Catholic.

JON: Are you through? Okay, let's go again from the top.

JON/OLGA: Father died just a year ago today
Your name day, Irina
The Fifth of May
The sky was muffled by falling snow
Softening the band's play
Just a year ago

Didn't think I'd survive the afternoon
You fainting, Irina
That corpse-like swoon
(LUKE *after prompting from* MATT, *whom* LUKE *has been playfully, mischievously trying to distract)*

LUKE/IRINA: Olga, why recall it?

LUKE: She fainted?

JON: You fainted, yes. You were overcome with grief at our father's death.

LUKE: You don't know my father

JON: Moving on.

JON/OLGA: And Masha mumbling our mother's name
Murmuring that old tune
Giving God the blame

MATT/MASHA: Snow falling
Sleet and heavy rain

LUKE/IRINA: Olga, I remember
My sweet, I'm
Not a scatterbrain

LUKE: They have that word in Russian?

JON: Luke! Why are you doing this?

LUKE: I can't keep it all straight.

JON: What?

LUKE: Just tell me what happens. I know, Jon. They
want to go to Moscow. Moscow 'til they puke. But
nothing happens. Nothing important.

JON: Nothing important, Luke. Just their lives.

LUKE: Well if it's so fucking important, why can't I
remember it? Just tell me again. Just the important
stuff.

JON: Okay.
(Overemphasizing the alliteration)
I'm Olga
I'm the oldest
I teach high school
I'm an old maid
You're Irina
You're the youngest
It's your name day

MATT: I'm Masha
In the middle
And I'm married
To Kuligan
And he teaches

At the high school
And I used to
Be his student

Now I wish I
Was his widow
I feel wasted

LUKE: Koo-lee who? Sounds like a French plumber.
Hey KOOL-EE-GAHN man!

MATT: Then along comes
My Vershinen
Whom we call the
Love-sick Major

JON: Who is married
With two daughters

MATT: Him we used to
Know in Moscow

JON: And whose wife is
Suicidal

MATT: Who adores me
As an equal
Even though it
Can't be bridal

JON: Who gets transferred
Off to Cracow
Or to somewhere
Else in Poland

MATT: And I fracture
Like a mirror
And I lose my
Chance at wholeness

JON: And we have a
Brother, Andrey
Whom we all thought
Would be something
But he marries
This Natasha

MATT & JON: And we hate her

LUKE: Why do you hate her?

JON: Because she's bourgeois.

LUKE: What does that mean?

JON: It means she's common, smug and greedy. Crass.

LUKE: Crass?

MATT: No class.

LUKE: Sounds like Jon.

MATT: Moving on.

JON: So he marries

This Natasha

LUKE: Wait! I know Natasha. Like in Bullwinkle. That's the first fuckin' Russky name I know. She wears black and has a deep voice. Deeper than Boris even. Hey, is there a Boris?

JON: There is no Boris. There is no Rocky. And whereas she has the same name, she is not the same character. Can you grasp that concept? Cartoon. Chekhov. Got it?

MATT: Moving on.

JON: Pretty soon she's
Taking over
And we're squeezed out
Of our own home
And our brother
Starts to gamble
And he squanders
All our money
So it's hardly

Any wonder
We're unhappy

LUKE: That's pretty crappy. But these broads started out unhappy. They been moanin' about Moscow since the first minute.

JON: At least you have a suitor. Two of them:

First there's
Tusenbach
The Baron
Whom you kind of
Like but pity
And Captain
Solyony
Who is rash and
Rather snitty
But adores you.

But Tusenbach
The Baron
Is the first to
Pop the question
And at first he
Gets the brush off
But then later
On you're desp'rate
So you say yes

You say yes when
He implores you
Making Solyony bitter
He is fitful
And he's jealous
Making life a
Bit more hellish
And more cruel

Because just when
You are fleeing
I mean finally escaping
And about to

Marry Baron
Captain kills your
Poor finance
In a duel

LUKE: Oh joy.

JON: Do you think you have that down now?

LUKE: Maybe vaguely.

JON: Can we go on.

LUKE: Do we have to?

JON: I will rip those socks into little cotton lint balls and scatter them across the stage like snowflakes on St. Petersburg, and we will never play sockball with you again. Do I make myself clear?

(LUKE nods)

JON: Okay. From the top.

LUKE: From the top?

JON: From. The. Top.

(Return to)

Chekhov's Opening

JON/OLGA: Father died just a year ago today
(Pulling LUKE's ear to try to get him to do his blocking)
Your name day, Irina
The fifth of May
The sky was muffled by falling snow
Softening the band's play
Just a year ago

Didn't think I'd survive the afternoon
You fainting, Irina
(A headlock on LUKE who will not do what JON wants)
That corpse-like swoon

LUKE/IRINA: *(Struggling)* Olga, why recall it?

JON/OLGA: *(Maintaining the headlock to keep him in place)*
And Masha mumbling our mother's name
Murmuring that old tune
Giving God the blame

MATT/MASHA: Snow falling
Sleet and heavy rain

LUKE/IRINA: *(Still struggling to break free)*
Olga, I remember
My sweet, I'm
Not a scatterbrain
(Finally escapes the headlock, gloating)
Today the sun is shining
No need to
Think of gloom again

JON/OLGA:
Now you blush with a joy you can't conceal
It's funny, Irina
How time can heal
Though truth abides in that old cliché
(Trying to get LUKE back in his grip)
Distancing our feelings
Won't keep them at bay

LUKE/IRINA: *(Keeping clear of JON and flaunting it)*
Olya, I don't deny the things you say
But call it perverseness
To feel this way
The sunlight is so gorgeous and we're alive
Bursting like a nosegay
Straining to survive

JON/OLGA:
(Grabbing LUKE by the crotch and pulling him into place)
Cut flowers cannot thrive, my love
Your simile is scary
I'm dampening your mood, my love
Don't mean to be contrary

I'm grateful for the sun today
Please don't think I'm not
I drink the light like wine today
Perhaps I am besot

(MASHA *has started to whistle softly or perhaps to say the* *word "whistle" during* JON's *above eight lines*)

JON/OLGA: Masha, please don't whistle

MATT/MASHA: Love, I'm only reading

JON/OLGA: It pierces like a thistle

MATT/MASHA: Does it sound so bleating

JON/OLGA: A chisel through my temple
Please do n't make my head ache
I'm still correcting lessons

LUKE/IRINA: Masha, please for godsake

(MATT *has managed to get* LUKE *settled down a bit to a* *point where* LUKE *is more playfully subversive and less* *belligerent*)

LUKE/IRINA: Olga, you're depressing
Open up a window
The birches look so pleasing
Blazing in the sun's glow

JON/OLGA: They're charred and cold and leafless, love
The branches aren't alive yet
In Moscow there are flowers, love
Asphodel and violet
Newborn scents and sweetness, 'Ri
Dogwood blooms and quince
Eleven years this spring it's been
We haven't been there since

Remember May in Moscow, love
O Masha you remember
The purple, red and yellow, love
While here could be December

You'll come each May to Moscow, love
And stay all through September
Even in high summer here
Life is monochrome
The sun's a sad pretender here
And I want to go home

LUKE/IRINA: I want to go home no less
You know I feel as you do
It's just the light today, I guess
And the air hums when I move through
And my heart feels like it used to
Maybe it's my name day
But you know I feel the same way

JON/OLGA: When will this ever end or
Will we be here forever
Irina you're so clever
See in to the future
Tell me we're returning

LUKE/IRINA: Love, there's no discerning
But today it seems that everything is nearer
The sky's so close that I could touch it
If I just knew how
And anything could happen
And the future seems clearer
We'll sell the house and pack our gray trunks
Make our brother a professor

MATT/MASHA: And dress my husband as a gray monk
Sell him off as a confessor
And I could move to Moscow
And not just for the summer
I could stay forever

JON/OLGA: Out of here forever

LUKE/IRINA: Three of us together

JON/OLGA: Leave here, go forever

LUKE/IRINA: Tomorrow go to Moscow

MATT/MASHA: Tomorrow make the grand 'scape

LUKE/IRINA: Tomorrow go to Moscow

JON/OLGA: See the flowers paint the landscape

LUKE/IRINA: Let the future save us somehow

MATT/MASHA: May the city spare us heartache

JON/OLGA: Pray the future takes us out of here
To Moscow

LUKE/IRINA: Moscow

MATT/MASHA: Moscow

(End of Chekhov's Opening)

LUKE: I am sick of fucking Moscow
I can't stand this fucking play
These three sisters suck the big one

JON: Okay, let's try the end of that again.

LUKE: I'll put this another way
I quit
I'm no longer saying
This shit.
(He exits.)

MATT: Do you think he was trying to tell us something?

JON: The little putz.

MATT: He's just being Irina.

JON: Irina is a sweet young kid who wants to do something with her life, make her mark, pull her load. The only load he wants to pull is in his pants. He's spoiled.

MATT: Irina's spoiled in her way. Every time she starts to work at something, she gets antsy. She has attention deficit disorder. Just like Luke.

JON: Oh she does, does she? Thank you, Uta. But he can't just walk off like that. It's a little different in here. When the going gets tough he can't just move to a new street corner and unzip his fly. Whether he likes it or not we are stuck in here together.

MATT: He's lost. I hear him sobbing sometimes when he thinks we're sleeping. He's lonely.

JON: If he's so goddam lonely why the hell did he just run out on us. Not that he can go anywhere. I'll give him something to sob about. No Chekhov, no sockball.

MATT: We can't do that to him.

JON: Of course we can.

MATT: He needs his sockball. As much as you need your Three Sisters—as much as I do. He'll come round. And when he does, we'll have our sister back.

And we can move to Moscow
And not just for the summer
We can stay forever

JON: Are you sure you've never acted before?

MATT: Only in my head. Do you like directing?

JON: I hate it. But somebody's gotta do it.

MATT: It doesn't seem like you hate it. Did you do it a lot? Back in your Greenwich Village days? You look like you know what you're doing.

JON: Playwrights think they know everything. I did it once before. Some trendy piece of shit we threw together at La Mama. Oh boy.

MATT: Who's we?

JON: We?

MATT: You said "we" — "we threw together at—La–Ma–Ma."

JON: What are you? A detective?

MATT: *(With a flourish:)* Masha Prozorov, private dick, at your service. *(Laughs, embarrassed, but exhilarated)* That's what I love about it in here. I could never have said that out there. I'd be too shy, too inhibited. *(Back to the point)* So who's we?

JON: The director and I. Mark. My lover at the time. Until he died in the middle of the second runthrough. Christ, he was something. A dynamo. Did everything. Designed the sets. Built them. Took the tickets. Played the lead. He'd know how to handle Luke. In more ways than one. Such fools we were. To be young, naive. Believe that art could change things.

MATT: You still believe that. Even in here. That's why you've given us *Three Sisters*.

JON: Chekhov gave *Three Sisters*.

MATT: They're your words.

JON: They're Chekhov's words.

MATT: Chekhov wrote in Russian. They're your words.

JON: Chekhov's ideas. Chekov's feelings.

MATT: Not just his. Not anymore. Yours too. You've given us a purpose. A play to do. This was an empty room. You made it a universe.

JON: It's an illusion. And it's not even mine. *(Beat. He laughs.)* I thought the theatre would be my life's work. Do I sound like Eve Harrington?

(JON tries to explain it all to MATT, jokey self-deprecating at first, then serious:)

Epiphany

JON: Playwrights think they're consecrated
But the job is overrated
We're never satisfied
Never gratified

For long
It's all too rarified

Just when you think that you're elated
You find that you're merely sated
For the moment
And that's an omen
Something's wrong

All this searching after truth's
A poor excuse to be uncouth
Phony
Without a Tony
To show for it
You blame yourself because you didn't go for it
Enough
Maybe you should have written
More fluff

Been more entertaining
A little cuter
Not so indulgent
Not so ridiculous
Less effulgent
More meticulous
Less sublime
Less bold or
At least more self-controlled or
Less afraid of getting older
What I want is more
Time

If I could balance the intensity
Of my insecurity
With the weight of my propensity
For artistic purity
Maybe I could feel fulfillment
This play could save me
I want the real fulfillment

Every smug achievement's
Always followed by bereavement, by pain
I want a satisfaction I can sustain
I don't want to slip again from joyous
To supercilious
From magnanimous
To bilious
Jesus Christ, I'm always redefining
It's so goddam undermining

It's all illusion
The theater is illusion
My whole life is illusion
It's all pretending
We search for truth
A constancy
The lies never ending
It's all a phony splendor
Not possible to render
Or regain
Illusions don't remain
They only fade
And the demons re-invade

There is no security
And not much continuity
That's how it's played
Connect the dots
Moment to moment
Line to line
Color in the spots
I need Three Sisters to be
A marvel, a wonder, an epiphany
An exultation, an exhortation, a sigh
But I'm afraid it will be
Another lie.

MATT: Not if I can help it. I love playing Masha. Do
you like playing Olga?

JON: Dried up fusty disapproving old Olga? Yeah. I think she suits me fine.

MATT: Olga's not like that. And you aren't either.

JON: Her life has slipped through her hands. And she's resigned to it.

MATT: You're not resigned. You're just like Vershinen.

JON: Vershinen? The lovesick major?

MATT: He speaks so sadly, just like you, with such remorse about his past, his sick wife, his little girls. How if he could live life over again he would do everything differently. How happiness is not possible in his lifetime. And yet here he is seeing the three sisters again and he is so delighted, so full of happiness. Such a contradiction. And Masha sees that and she's drawn to him. He saves her.

JON: Saves her? When he leaves her, doesn't that destroy her?

MATT: Destroy her? He's brought her back to life.

JON: Only to die again.

MATT: You don't know that. I don't know yet what happens after the curtain comes down.

JON: But she's devastated.

MATT: Devastated maybe, but not destroyed! He's given her something that even his leaving can't take away. *(Slight pause)* It's easier to talk about our characters than to talk about ourselves, isn't it?

JON: I had a professor who used to say we always think of ourselves as characters anyway. The face we show the world is always a construct of our own devising. I protested vehemently at the time. Now I fear he may be right.

MATT: Is that so fearsome?

JON: It's sad.

MATT: The self always shows through. Just like when you peek out of Olga. Or the Baron. Or Vershinen!

JON: Will you cut it out already with that Vershinen stuff. I am further from him than any of them. He's a soldier, for godsake. So straight-backed. So confident. So poised.

MATT: And? Where's the problem?

JON: Me? Hello? He's capable of falling swimmingly boyishly greenly in love. No way. Give me Olga any day. Our salad days are over. Hell, our meat and potato days are over.

MATT: Oh, my lord. You are a funny man. You don't think you could ever say the things Vershinen says to Masha?

JON: Not anymore. What things?

MATT: In their love scene.

JON: You mean:

(He is embarrassed but having fun as a bombasticly dashing Vershinen)
"You glorious luminous creature
Though you cool your face in darkness
Your eyes still glow with fire
Tell my why"

MATT: *(As a coy MASHA)*
"Dusk can fall on us so sharply
I'll turn the lamplight higher
But not too high"

Come on. You can say it—

JON: *(Plunging in as Vershinen)*
"I love you,
I love you,
I love you,

I love my smile inside your eyes,
The way you tilt your head — "

Oh for godsake, I sound like Margaret Thatcher on
ecstacy.

MATT: Go on!

JON: *(Even more fun)*
"The way you try to make me feel
You've soaked up every word I've said
There is splendor in your shadow
There is wonder in the way you wrap your stole
The way you shrug your shoulder
Just let me touch your shoulder—
Just touch your shoulder—
Just touch your shoulder—"

Oh puh-leeze. I'm making myself puke.

MATT: "When you talk like that
It makes me laugh
Although I'm frightened
Please don't repeat it
Well you can say it if you mean it
But not too loud
But not so soft that I don't hear it
I need to hear it
So I laugh more
I need to laugh more
So I don't mind it
If you do mean it
But come a little nearer
So I can hear or
See if you mean it"

JON: Beautifully done. On your part. Just the right
balance of melancholy and lust. Thank God I'm dried
up fusty disapproving ol' Olga.

MATT: You make a wonderful Vershinen. Do you think Masha knows going in that he'll never leave his wife and the girls?

JON: I don't know. But I'm sure *you* have an opinion.

MATT: I do. I think she knows.

JON: You do? That's it doomed? That she's going to have her heart broken?

MATT: Yes, I do. She thinks it's worth it. To feel alive after so many years of death. That's Masha. Yes.

JON: You know her so well.

MATT: She reminds me of my mother.

JON: Really?

MATT: She was stuck in a place she hated too.

JON: Where was that?

MATT: You won't believe it.

JON: Try me.

MATT: *(Pronouncing it Mosc-oh)* Mosco.

JON: Moscow?!

MATT: Mosc-oh. That's how she pronounced it anyway.

JON: Where the hell is that?

MATT: Somewhere.

JON: Don't be coy with me, young man. Where is it?

MATT: Idaho.

JON: Idaho?! They have black people in Idaho?

MATT: Well we weren't native.

Mosco, Idaho

MATT: Detroit, my Mom grew up in Motown
I guess it was a letdown
To find yourself in Idaho
God forbid
The place can be an albatross
If you think you're Diana Ross
And Jesus knows, my mother did

She pretended freely
She'd come home from the cannery
She'd sweep me up and carry me
It's my oldest memory
And we'd run out through Main Street
I'd shake just like a tambourine
And when we got to Friendship Square
She'd do an old Supreme's routine
And dance like a millionaire

She'd say
I miss my Motor City life
I swear to God I'll never stay
Idaho's a Conway Twitty life
And Detroit is Marvin Gaye

But poor Mom
She met my father
He was a Nez Pierce Indian
Who never knew he had a son
He died a drunk at twenty one
Guess it was too much bother
To make it back to Michigan
From Idaho with me in tow
And her big plans came all undone

So how
How do you find you way home now?
When you move only forward on a single track
And never in reverse

Detroit's no longer Motown
Detroit's a dream, that makes it worse
Than even Mosco, Idaho
That's really why we never did go
Back

I miss my mother
I miss our singing
Like the old Supremes
I even miss those silly
Dance routines
I miss Mosco Main Street
And where it ends at Friendship Square

Without the past we're incomplete
And sometimes when it's hard to bear
I think of Momma and the cool night air
Me clapping hands and cooing harmony
In Friendship Square
The lightning bugs lit up like phosphorous
At twilight when there's no one there
But us

JON: *(To* MATT*)* You—

(LUKE *enters with broom handle and sockball.)*

LUKE: You done here? I want to hit some sockballs.

JON: Play in the lobby.

LUKE: It's not big enough.

JON: Story of your life.

LUKE: Fuck you.

JON: Poor Princess Little Meat. Could be a liability for a street hustler. You had to make ends meet somehow. What's a boy to do fresh off the bus from Mobile, mouth open, legs apart?

MATT: I think I'm going to have my dressing room redecorated. *(He exits.)*

JON: No, Matt! Stay-—

LUKE: *(Overlapping* JON*)* Hey. Don't go. Hang around.
Matt? *(He starts to toss the sockball and hit it with the
broom handle.)*

JON: We have such an uneasy peace in here. I'd hate to
see it broken.

LUKE: Why does this shit matter to you so much? It's
only a play.

JON: So it's been said.

LUKE: And not a very good one.

JON: No? You don't like my translation?

LUKE: You should change the names. Make 'em more
American. I've never heard of those names.

JON: Irina? That's Irene. Surely there was an Irene in
that Alabama hog holler from whence you sprang.

LUKE: Why didn't you make it Irene then. That's what
I mean. And nothing ever happens. Just a lot of talk.
About stuff that never happens. It's not very good.

JON: But it's their lives.

LUKE: Well they're not very good lives. The coolest
thing in it is that duel and we never even get to see it. It
happens off screen.

JON: Stage. It happens off stage.

LUKE: You should spice it up a little. Bring that duel
on screen—stage. Make it between Irene and Auggie.
Maybe then I'd be interested. You and me, we could
have ourselves a duel. With swords. *(Brandishing the
broom handle)* I'd put you out of your misery.

JON: I can't change it. And I don't think Olga translates
very well as Auggie.

LUKE: Sure you can change it, it's not exactly the Holy
Bible now, is it?

JON: No. It's better. It's Chekov.

LUKE: It's a bunch of letters. And some are backwards. And some have little squiggles. How do we know they say what you say they say?

JON: I know Russian.

LUKE: How do I know? You could be making us say whatever you want us to say.

JON: Why would I do that?

LUKE: Because you like to control things.

JON: If I were going to make things up, why would I give you and Matt all the best parts?

LUKE: The best parts? You kiddin' me?

JON: You get to be restless, idealistic, fickle, *young*. Or you would. If you hadn't quit.

LUKE: I'm young already.

JON: Oh for godsake. And I get to be the old maid headmistress.

LUKE: If you don't like your part, why are you so *gung ho* to rehearse it all the time?

JON: Don't you understand?

LUKE: Understand what? That we've been trapped inside a theatre for we don't even know how long? And we don't know if we're dead or alive or if there's an outside anymore. And we don't know why we're here or how it happened that we got here in the first place? Of course I don't understand.

JON: You don't understand why we do *Three Sisters*?

LUKE: No. No I don't.

JON: Because it's something to do. It gives order to our days. Parameters.

LUKE: What's that?

JON: Boundaries. Structure.

LUKE: That's not good enough.

JON: That's all there is. Us, this theatre, this play. By some accident, there was a book left here—alone—with us in this theater.

LUKE: How likely is that?

JON: It happened to be a play—a Russian play. I happen to know Russian—

LUKE: How likely is that?

Likely

JON: Likely?
Oh that's exquisite
How likely is it
That we are here?

Highly
Highly unlikely
The world around us
Could disappear

Somehow
Somehow it's happened
So what is likely
Is not so clear

Luke there aren't any answers
God's a phantom puppeteer
Likelihood is hard to come by
It's an old world souvenir
(Getting an idea with which to make fun of LUKE*)*
Likely
Sounds like a stage name
Appearing nightly
On the marquee

Likely
The famed Luke Likely

Luke Likely's in it
We have to see

Critics
Are creaming daily
And Army Archerd's
Your devotee

Liz Smith
Is doing backflips
And for sheer raving
I quote Rex Reed:

"Anton Chekhov writes Three Sisters
Stanislavksy's turning green
Luke Likely performs Irina
No, Luke Likely *is* Irene."

LUKE: You are an asshole.

JON: I suppose you're right. Still. Luke Likely. That is the best made-up name since Holly Golightly.

LUKE: Is that some drag queen?

JON: Truman Capote? Breakfast at Tiffany's.

LUKE: Was that the drag queen's real name? Truman? Because I know Tiffany's a drag queen name.

JON: Oh for godsake. If you outlive me how will gay culture survive. Truman Capote was the author. Holly Golightly was his creation, a character in his novella.

LUKE: You think I might live longer than you?

JON: If I don't accidentally decapitate you first.

LUKE: Then you think we're alive?

JON: Oh god, Luke, haven't you thrashed this one around enough?

LUKE: You think God made a mistake?

JON: Which time?

LUKE: Putting us here.

JON: Okay. Going along with your God premise—for the moment. How so?

LUKE: Maybe one of us was supposed to be a woman.

JON: A woman?

LUKE: To continue the race. If there were a woman here, we could make babies.

JON: I suppose we could. If we had to. I don't see any turkey basters around, but we could. Maybe we're all three God's mistakes. Maybe there are a couple of breeders in another theater somewhere with Mary Martin's copy of *I Do, I Do*.

LUKE: But if they are, then why are we here?

JON: So the only reason to be alive is to procreate the race.

LUKE: If you're the only people alive it is.

JON: I don't buy that. If God wants a new race let Him start from scratch. I'm here to do *Three Sisters*.

LUKE: So there's no reason.

JON: I just told you. We're here to do *Three Sisters*. That's our reason. We're here so we can want to do to Moscow.

LUKE: God doesn't care about Moscow. That's not a reason.

JON: Why does there have to be another reason?

LUKE: Because if there's no other reason then we are probably dead and this is probably hell.

JON: Probably? You mean likely? Hey you're Luke Likely ain'tcha? You play Irene in that *Three Sisters* show, don'tcha? You sure are convincin'! Can I have your autograph? *Who knows?* Heaven? Hell? *Krypton!* Who cares?

LUKE: I care. God wouldn't just let this happen to us. For no reason.

JON: What if God had nothing to do with it?

LUKE: You sound like the devil.

JON: Luke. *(In a Darth Vader voice)* Luke. Come to the dark side, Luke. It is your destiny.

LUKE: Oh cut it out. Fuck you. Fuck you.

JON: God cries when you talk like that, Luke.

LUKE: I said cut it out.

JON: Maybe he caught you wanking off one time too many.

LUKE: I said stop it. Stop it.

JON: Go ahead hit me.

LUKE: You're such a fucking old queen, who can't take anything serious. For godsake, if you can't take this serious, what can you take serious?

JON: I take *Three Sisters* serious-*ly*.

LUKE: Fuck *Three Sisters*.

JON: There's procreation for you. *(He exits.)*

LUKE: You snotty pussy jerk-off! Go hide behind your Chehkov. Go hide behind your pussy play!

(LUKE pitches the sockball wildly, hitting MATT as MATT enters.)

MATT: Practicing your fastball?

LUKE: I didn't mean to get uncool on you like that before.

MATT: Wanna just play catch?

LUKE: Sure.

MATT: Where is Jon?

LUKE: I don't know. Probably peeling the paint off the walls with his teeth. Who is this Chekov anyway? Jon makes like he's God or something. Maybe Jon made him up too. It's such an ego trip for him. I think he really gets off on it.

MATT: You get off on sockball.

LUKE: I like watching you play. I like the way your body moves. Jon's a mess. Were you ever a dancer?

MATT: No! Jon will get better. Never as good as you, of course. But better. He'll start to enjoy it. So will you, in the play. If you would come back. Stick with it.

LUKE: Are you pimpin' for him?

MATT: Pimping. How colorful. No. I'm not pimping.

LUKE: Doesn't it bother you that we are trapped here?

MATT: I don't feel trapped.

LUKE: But why, Matt? Why? What are we doing here?

MATT: I don't think about it.

LUKE: How can you not?

Becoming Me

MATT: Luke it's kinda funny
Since we've been inside here
I feel more alive here
I still don't know what here is
But somehow I belong
Luke, I feel I'm right here
And I used to feel so wrong

As far back as I remember
I was this scrawny little boy
Without a father
Without a reason

With a mother who was crazy
Who tried her best but was unable

Sometimes we simply are unable
I know

But I feel safe here
And I feel able
I don't feel scrawny
Or worse—unstable
It's all alright here
It's all okay
Matthew's come to Moscow
He's found his way

And though Moscow's still a mystery
Still a cryptogram
I have reconciled my history
And I begin to know
Who I am

And all my sorrow
And all my joy
And all my Mama's dreams
And that still scrawny boy
Begin to quiet
Begin to dim
And I can hear myself

And I can see
That somehow coming here
Was meant to be
Because by coming here
I'm becoming free
And by becoming free
I'm becoming
Me

LUKE: And that's enough?

MATT: For me. I play sockball. I play Masha.

LUKE: I have to get out of here.

MATT: So like Irina. Growing ever more desperate to escape. You could put all that fire into Irina. All that searching.

LUKE: Why?

MATT: Because you might find some release. Some peace.

LUKE: She's only a made-up person in a play.

MATT: Who want and needs as you do. She wants to escape too. She's dreaming dreams of Moscow.

LUKE: I don't understand that Moscow shit.

MATT: If that stage door opened—and there was a Harley out there—waiting for you, where would you go?

LUKE: I guess there's Alabama, but I can't go back there.

MATT: Screw the past, Luke, it's just a prison! Come on now, Luke, work with me.

A window opens, Luke, you're free
The world is new and all's forgiven
Where do you go? What will you be?
Hop on your Harley—

Alabama

LUKE: Okay I'm sitting
On a cycle
On a highway
Just like that movie
From Ted Turner
On the T V
With Bridget Fonda's father
That tan old lady's brother
Not the grandpa

MATT: You're thinking Peter

LUKE: *(Taking it sexually)* What!?

MATT: Her brother's name is Peter

LUKE: Oh!

MATT: And the movie's Easy Rider

LUKE: *(Overlapping)* —Rider, Easy Rider

MATT: So you're sitting on a cycle

LUKE: God, there sure are lotsa Fondas

MATT: Could we kindly get beyond this
So you're sitting
On a cycle
On a highway

LUKE: I'm kinda "fonda" that idea
'cept I wanna skip that old guy
With me I've got Martina
For an old girl she's got great thighs
Thighs to wrap around a Harley

MATT: Martina?

LUKE: You know, like tennis

You know, like backhand

MATT: Oh

LUKE: And Greg Louganis

MATT: Oh

LUKE: You know, like high dive
You know, like back flip
You know, that backside -——

On a Harley
I can hardly
Keep my hard on
In my blue jeans

MATT: *(As* LUKE *grabs* MATT'*s hips from behind)* Luke!

LUKE: We head for Mobile
With the Olympic torch
We pass through Hoke's Bluff
Right by my father's porch

Alabama's in a frenzy
The crimson tide turns pink
See the klansman in his bed sheet
He don't know what to think

When we take the field there's a hiss
I get jumpy, try to mask it
From second base, Greg blows me a kiss
See the klansman blow a gasket

I've come home to Alabama
With Greg Louganis and Martina
Navratilova-—
Hey is she Russian
Is that a Russian name
It sounds like Russian
The names all sound the same—

In the ninth we're sittin' pretty
Greg has scored one run
I've been pitching a no hitter
So it's zip to one

When their designated hitter
Smacks my curve ball
It's a homer sure as shootin'
Out the ball park
But Martina's at the back wall
And those great thighs
I mean this dyke flies

And it's all over
Yeah it's their third out
And then that quiet
And then this great shout

And they're screaming for Martina
And they're stomping on the bleachers
And they're yelling for Louganis
And they're ripping off his jersey
And he's howling "where's the pitcher?"

And he grabs me
And then he hugs me
Without his jersey

And I feel safe now
And I feel right now
And I feel saved now
And I feel light now
In Alabama
If it were Moscow

MATT: Stick with it.

LUKE: And the moon looks like a baseball
And the bases swarm the Milky Way
And Martina, Greg and me say
So long now
And mount our Harleys
Except for Greg
So he climbs aboard behind me

MATT:	LUKE:
And all my sorrow	And he kicks up the pedal
And all my joy	And I feel shiny
And all my Mama's dreams	And I feel golden
And that still scrawny boy	And maybe it's my medal
Begin to quiet	Or him behind and holdin' me
And I feel safe here	Just him behind and holdin' me
And I feel right here	And I feel safe now
And I feel saved here	And I feel right now
And I feel light here	And I feel saved now
I know that coming here	And I feel light now

Was meant to be   In Alabama
And now I see   If this were Moscow
Because by coming here
I'm becoming me

MATT: That wasn't so hard, was it?

LUKE: Harder than you know. It's not good to pretend about things you can never have. Or be. How'd you know I like a Harley?

MATT: A lucky guess.

LUKE: I always wanted one of my own. A black one. Feel all that power between my legs.

MATT: Oh yeah.

LUKE: An older guy I used to see had one. And he would pick me up and tool me around. He was a movie executive at Disney. I wasn't suppose to know that, but I saw his name in the credits at the end of Pocohantas. It gave me an erection.

MATT: Seeing his name at the end of Pocohantas?

LUKE: No, riding around with him on the Harley.

MATT: Oh.

LUKE: Like now.

MATT: Harley's can be fun.

LUKE: Do you ever get lonely in here?

MATT: No. So will you come back? To us? To Jon's play?

LUKE: My Daddy used to say play-acting was the devil's work.

MATT: Is that what you believe?

LUKE: Maybe.

MATT: Your father sounds very religious.

LUKE: *(No self-pity, much humor)* Oh yeah. My Daddy was a Baptist minister. And he believed in two things. God and baseball. I sat in the front pew of his church every Sunday. And every Thursday and every Saturday he sat with me on the bench for my ball games. I was good. Real good. And he was very proud of me. In his way. 'Til he caught me goin' down on a colored boy when I was fourteen. He picked up his bible and my baseball bat and chased me out of the house. Hell he chased me out of the county.

MATT: And you mother just stood by and let him?

LUKE: My momma died when I was born. When my Daddy was runnin' down the road after me, he said it was an abomination that my momma should have to die givin' birth to a lil' nigger-lovin' faggot like me.

MATT: When you were fourteen?!

LUKE: I'm not so stupid, I went to high school for awhile. And I did real well too. We didn't study that Chekhov dude. But we read. Catcher in the Rye. I loved that. And Lord of the Flies. Which is kinda like here almost. My English teacher was a big old dyke. She was great. She liked me. A lot. Do you?

MATT: *(Teasing)* I'd like you more if you'd do *Three Sisters* with us.

LUKE: How can that be so important to you?

MATT: It could be important to you if you'd give it a chance.

LUKE: I could be important to you if you gave me a chance.

MATT: You are important to me.

LUKE: Am I?

MATT: Yes. And I am giving you a chance. Work with us.

LUKE: Come on. You know that's not what I mean.

Touch

LUKE: I'm maybe not all that you'd want
Maybe not what you'd want at all
Out there
But in here
I'm a warm body
And I can be tender

MATT: Luke—

LUKE: Maybe not what you'd want
But you could pretend or
I could play rough or
I could just hold you
Or I could just suck you
Or do what you told me
Or you could just fuck me

MATT: Luke, please don't talk like that.

LUKE: If you would just touch me
Anywhere
Or just let me touch you
Anywhere
Just touch your shoulder

MATT: Luke—

LUKE: I'm maybe not all that you'd want
But who ever is that
I know I'm not all that you want
But who ever is, Matt?
I'm a warm body
I can be tender
I can play tough or
I could surrender
If you would just touch me
We could be
Anywhere

But here
Or just let me touch you
I'll take you
Anywhere

MATT: Please, stop—

LUKE: If you don't soon touch me
I think I'll go crazy
Oh Matt I'm so lonely
In here

You don't have to listen
Pretend that I'm lying
I thought we were dead, Matt
Now I feel like I'm dying

MATT: Oh Luke, no—

LUKE: Okay I'm not all that you want
But who ever is that
There's got to be something you want
Just say what it is, Matt

MATT: It can't be like this, Luke.

LUKE: You don't have to love me
You don't have to need me
If you would just touch me
Or just let me hold you
Just touch your shoulder
First just your shoulder

MATT: I can't, Luke.

LUKE: You can't now or you can't ever?

MATT: I can't.

(Long pause)

(LUKE exits, leaving MATT stunned and confused.)

(MATT is left alone on stage for a long time.)

JON: Matt?

MATT: Hi—

JON: Are you alright?

MATT: Luke...Luke just...

JON: He'll drive you nuts.

MATT: I feel like...someone just...

JON: He leaves you speechless, doesn't he?

MATT: You... It's nice to see you.

JON: You just saw me.

MATT: You know what I'm thinking just now, seeing you?

JON: No.

MATT: *(As a romantic amazed Vershinen)*
"Look at all the flowers in this room!
It's such a wondrous place.
Half my life have I spent scraping
Round from room to empty room
And here this room's been waiting
All I've been missing
These flowers blooming
This room here waiting"

After all that dreary philosophizing in the first act you—I'm sorry: Vershinen—suddenly bursts up out of his chair in the middle of one of the Baron's starchy harangues and says, "Look at all the flowers in this room". That's what you make me think. It's my favorite speech in the play.

JON: Really?

MATT: Maybe I was wrong about Masha.

JON: How?

MATT: Maybe she does believe going in that there's a chance at happiness. A chance that he'll leave his family. A chance for them to have a life. Maybe she really believes she can have him.

JON: Maybe she does. But Vershinen on the other hand, surely he knows it's impossible.

MATT: Maybe for a moment he is inflamed by her fire.

(MATT *goes to touch* JON's *shoulder.*)

JON: And fools himself?

(JON *intercepts* MATT's *hand.*)

I'm glad you like that speech. Even if it is just a translation. That means a lot to me. Thank you.

(JON *exits.*)

(*Lights dim.*)

Empty Room

MATT: You're in an empty room
You watch him walk away
The barren walls would bloom
If he would only stay
You feel the future loom
And yet it's held at bay

And you're left grasping
Masha, close your hand
It's only air your clasping
Don't give into blindness
Save yourself the lashing
He's uncouth and spineless
You deserve a dashing

Man, fill your mouth with mine
Don't try to justify
Twist me to serpentine
Your lips will sanctify
Me, turn my blood to wine

I'll try to satisfy
You like a lover

Lover, let me run
My cheek across your stubble
Stop my soul from aching
Help me to discover
How to keep from breaking
Like a flimsy bubble

You're in an empty room
You watch him walk away
The barren walls would bloom
If he would only stay
Forever

(MATT *is still, his hand outstretched.*)

(*Play should be performed without an intermission, in which case:* MATT *composes himself after singing* Empty Room. *Lights brighten very gradually.* LUKE *enters with sockball and broom handle.* JON *enters opposite with the Chekhov text and curtain swatches for costumes. They both offer their props to* MATT *as if to say "choose me."* MATT *"chooses"* JON'*s pastime, and they both turn to* LUKE.)

(*If performed with an intermission, perhaps the lights fade slowly on* MATT *after he sings* Empty Room. *And when the audience returns from the interval they find the men engaged in another game of sockball, as in the opening. This time the game is perhaps more somber.*)

JON: It's time.

(*They begin to prepare for a runthrough of a new* Three Sisters *scene set in a bedroom, rearranging the trunk and foot stool.* JON *places the broom handle on the floor to denote a window. They perform the ritual flourish of their costume cloth and don their Three Sister's garb. The lights warm, redder than before.* LUKE *and* MATT *exit, leaving* JON *as* OLGA *alone on stage*)

Chekhov's Fire Scene

LUKE/IRINA: *(Entering with news)*
The Vershinen house was nearly burnt to cinders
But the breeze blew back the blaze to Lyov Creek

MATT/MASHA: *(Entering with more news)*
His girls are huddled underneath the staircase
Where Irina used to play at hide-and-seek

JON/OLGA:
Make sure they're bundled up, that's such a cold place
Did you get the little one to speak?

MATT/MASHA:
She said she feared her father was on fire
She said she saw a scarecrow once in flames
The older one just rocks her, strokes her forehead
I wish I could remember both their names

LUKE/IRINA:
And their mother
Did you hear her?
All that howling
She nearly
Hit Natasha
On the chin
Natasha
Fled the room and
Took to scowling
Avoiding
Her since Major
Brought her in

MATT/MASHA:
If Natasha
Weren't so evil
To begin with
I'd say that
She had met her
Evil twin

LUKE/IRINA:
That's hardly
Being fair to
Dame Vershinen
Natasha
Makes that crazy
Look a saint

The Baron says
Our brother's wife's
Been sinning
She lets the mayor
Dip his brush
In Andrey's paint

JON/OLGA: You mustn't listen to the Baron
When he's drinking
And that expression—one can hardly
Call it quaint

LUKE/IRINA: I've heard the same things whispered
At the council
You're so naïve—it makes me
Want to faint

MATT/MASHA: Listen to the two of you
What are you thinking
She's ridden roughshod over you
To everything she asks you acquiesce
She makes you share this tiny bedroom
To make room for our nephew
Who may not be our nephew
Who can guess

JON/OLGA: Masha, please, sister
The fire has upset you
I don't doubt it
Don't let it
I beseech you
Don't speak so freely

MATT/MASHA: 'Rina's right, you're so naïve
Look how you've settled
Your mouths are mealy
You teachers
Just like my husband
Once I think he loved you
He'd be better having loved you
Than loving me

LUKE/IRINA: *(Andrey's violin music is heard)*
Listen—
Please don't argue
I couldn't bear it
Just listen
It's Andrey—
I'm sorry
For ever bringing up
Natasha
It's just that—
Oh listen

JON/OLGA: Andrey and his violin

MATT/MASHA: We thought he would be our hero

JON/OLGA: A professor, in Moscow

MATT/MASHA: Now hear how he's broken

LUKE/IRINA: All that gossiping at work

MATT/MASHA: Now he's fiddling like Nero

JON/OLGA: And dreaming of Moscow

MATT/MASHA: Now hear how he's buckled

LUKE/IRINA: Resigned to be the Mayor's clerk

MATT/MASHA: And also his cuckold

LUKE/IRINA: Look out the window
The fire is flaring
It must be a silo
And all that dry wheat

JON/OLGA: The night's getting colder
In spite of the heat
I feel ten years older

MATT/MASHA: Oh look, in the street
Isn't it the mayor?
Coming here to pay her
A visit

LUKE/IRINA: And the violin
Keeps playing

MATT/MASHA: Exquisite

JON/OLGA: And here comes
Vershinen

MATT/MASHA: Oh—is it?

LUKE/IRINA: Why did Papa
Make Andrey
And me learn Italian?

JON/OLGA: Remember that tutor
Oh what a rapscallion

LUKE/IRINA: *(Spluttering out of control)*
Andrey stop playing
And look out your window
Caro fratello, guarda la—
Oh God, I've forgotten
What was the Italian
*(Distractedly, accidentally knocking over the footsool and
kicking the broken broom handle window marker)*
I can't remember
The Italian for window
And everyday I—

JON: Okay. Okay. It's getting away from us. Let's
regroup. I don't think we're ready for the next section
just yet.

LUKE: You mean it's getting away from me.

JON: No. All of us. There's a lot going on right here. We're halfway through the play. They—we have been stuck here in the boondocks for eleven years and we're all starting to come apart in different ways. So—let's not lose connection with the subtext. What are we thinking at this point. What are we feeling. *(To* LUKE*)* Alright. Don't edit. Let's hear the interior monologue.

LUKE: *(Clueless)* Wha—?

JON: *(To explain)* What is Irina thinking?

LUKE: I don't know what she's thinking. Can't I just go on?

JON: Go on where?

LUKE: From where you stopped me:
I can't remember
The Italian for window
And every day I
Forget someth—

JON: How can you do that speech when you don't know what's going on underneath it? She's not fumbling for an Italian word, she's mourning the passing of an entire way of life. Okay, let's start simpler. Tell me about Irina's new job at the town council. What is it doing to her? And try to connect with what you're saying. Go ahead.

LUKE/IRINA: *(He does an over-the-top hillbilly take on this.)*
If I could only laugh
Instead I want to spit
At first the telegraph
I thought that that was it
But this is worse by half
Again I swear I'll quit

But this time quicker
Olya, bare my back
And thrash me with a wicker

If I work tomorrow
The councilmen grow thicker
I'd rather dig potatoes—

JON: *(Furious, cutting him off in the middle of the second verse)* What the hell to you think you're doing!? Don't make fun of her! She feels trapped and wasted where she is! How do you like it in here?

LUKE: You know fucking well how I like it in here.

JON: I want to hear that. In the words. Pretend I'm an alderman. Give it to me. I'm your boss- I'm the Mayor! Come at me. Go for it. Now.

LUKE: Now?

JON: Now! Right now. Go back to the text. Come on.

LUKE: I don't want-—

JON: *(Shoving LUKE, to provoke him)* I SAID NOW!

LUKE/IRINA: *(He begins, using the song to get at JON, JON prods him heatedly interjecting "come on", "yes", "that's it")*
I write down every word
Of every alderman
I read them back unheard
I want to poke my pen

(JON provokes him with an attempted swipe)

LUKE/IRINA: In each inflated bird
And make each cock a hen

(LUKE has caught JON's arm as they struggle with one another.)

LUKE/IRINA: Then no more jargon
I'd slit their tongues
And mute them in the bargain
No more foolish nonsense
And such easy targets
(Maybe he has pinned JON and covers his mouth.)

A simple end to pretense
And such blessed silence
(*Almost deranged, strangling* JON *by the end*)
I've lost my mind I fear
From wanting something more
I've lost another year
I'm nearly twenty-four
And wasted—

There. Is that what you wanted? You are one sick fuck.
(*He exits, unhinged*)

JON: He's finally getting it, huh?

MATT: Do you think it's wise to push him that hard?

JON: What's to be gained if he just walks through it? It
has to mean something to him. Otherwise we might as
well just play sockball or go off into our own isolated
corners like hermits. Or fuck like animals until we're
raw and we forget what it's like to be human. This
world has no structure unless we believe in one. And
without a structure this world will collapse on us like
an imploding star.

MATT: So now it's not enough that he play the play. He
has to believe too?

JON: Sometimes. In the heat of it. Yes. He has to give
himself over to belief.

MATT: He's not ready to do that. He's just a boy.

JON: Who has seen more of life than you have.

MATT: Maybe so. Maybe all the more reason that he's
not ready. Maybe all the more reason not to push him.

JON: Oh for godsake, Matt, it was just a little acting
exercise.

MATT: He is having enough trouble just being here.
The play should be a refuge for him. A sanctuary.

JON: It would be if he gave himself over to it honestly.

MATT: He doesn't know how to do that yet and it's unfair of you to ask him.

JON: You sound like his mother.

MATT: Is that so bad? The kid's never had a mother. You sound like his father, ready to disown him when he can't do what you want.

JON: I thought you saw things the way I did.

MATT: I'm just asking you to be gentler with him. After all, he's come back to us. He knows he needs us. That's an awful lot of power to have over anyone. Wield it gently. Do you really think that we'd wander off to our own corners in isolation like hermits? That would truly be hell.

JON: I don't know what we might do if we didn't have something to hold on to.

MATT: We might fuck like animals until we were raw and forget what it's like to be human.

JON: And that would be a grave mistake.

MATT: Do you think fucking makes you forget what it's like to be human?

JON: I think it can. Without a framework.

MATT: A framework? You mean like love. Or affection.

JON: Sex is a can of worms. A Pandora's—pardon the express—box. Better left unopened here. Surely you see that.

MATT: I wouldn't know.

JON: You mean —

MATT: Yes.

JON: Never?

MATT: Never.

JON: Just with yourself?

MATT: No. I mean I've had dreams, you know. But never awake.

JON: Never awake? How do you get to sleep in the first place.

MATT: I try to remember the songs my mother used to make up in Idaho. She always sang me to sleep when I was a kid.

JON: You are something else.

MATT: A virgin? I think sex is a part of what makes us truly human.

JON: I think so too. That isn't what I meant. I was just being my usual hyperbolic self. I said "fucking 'til we're raw:" letting it consume us. In here. It would be dangerous.

MATT: Have you ever done that? Let it consume you?

JON: On occasion.

MATT: Do you miss it?

JON: No. No! Absolutely not.

MATT: I know it's not very Chekovian to talk about sex.

JON: No, it's not.

MATT: Do you think Masha and Vershinen ever consummated their relationship?

JON: I think they respect their circumstances more than that.

MATT: Their marriages? Doesn't that make them as convention-ridden as my husband? Isn't that what I hate so much?

JON: No. No, they're different. Romantic certainly. Wildly so. But ultimately platonic. Surely you agree.

MATT: I don't know. I haven't found the answer yet.

(Pause)

Is there anything I can do for you?

JON: Hmmm?

MATT: Before I retire. Rub your temples? Pull down your bed?

JON: That's what I miss: a mattress! No. I'm fine. Try to sleep.

MATT: You too. If you have trouble I can try one of my mother's lullabies on you.

JON: I don't think I'll have trouble tonight.

MATT: *(Desperately grasping* JON's *hand, kissing it)* Jon…

JON: I've reached a watershed
It's coming calmly clear
I've made an empty bed
I've made the rules in here
All I once was is dead
Or soon to disappear

Without a glimmer
Masha, fetch a glass
And catch me in the mirror
We can watch me fading
See the phantom flimmer
End the masquerading
Sink the drowning swimmer

(JON *gently sends* MATT *away.* MATT *exits.*)

JON: Matthew, don't remind me
Of all I've put behind me…

Behind Me

Behind me
The world goes on behind me
I'm sitting on the southern shore
Of Fire Island

I'm pondering the natural lure
Of Fire Island
I've walked up through the pines
Before me
The horizon waits before me
Unchanging for a million years
The constellations
Their stars undimmed by earthly fears
A consolation
And I draw in the lines

Behind me
The boys dance on behind me
They're coupling in the grass
I'd see the moonlight
Reflected off a naked ass
White as the moonlight
If I'd turn round behind

Around me
They all dance on around me
Their siren song surrounds me
The minutes and the years
The living and the dead
But I close off my ears
And I raise up my head

Behind me
I've put the past behind me
I won't let them remind me
Of all I've given up
The loving and the lust
The always empty cup
The lovers turned to dust

Behind me
I've put it all behind me
Moscow is behind me
Before me

The future is before me
Life goes on before me
Behind me
It all goes on inside me
Behind me
I want someone beside me
The world goes on inside me
My life goes on inside me
Inside me
Before me is behind me
Inside me

(LUKE *appears behind* JON.)

JON: Satan get behind me
Behind me
Behind me

(LUKE *approaches* JON *from behind.* MATT *enters opposite
in shadows and watches unseen by the other two.*)

JON: Lover get behind me
Behind me
Behind me

(LUKE *seduces* JON. *As this occurs it moves upstage, then
off.* MATT *takes stage and sings as if to block out what
he knows is happening. At times perhaps he does an old
Supremes-style dance routine.*)

So Long, Matt

MATT: So long, Matt
You move today, Matt
You got away, Matt
From Idaho, boy
You gotta go, boy

I wish you luck, Matt
Though you won't need it
Your future's set, Matt
I've placed my bet, Matt

Your star is shining
It shines like Venus
And though the miles, son
Will be between us
I'll feel your light, child
To warm my night, child
And nights get cold, boy
In Idaho, boy

Do you remember
We'd make up dances
Pretend there's spotlights
And colored gobos
We had a name too
The Idahobos

We'd run through Main Street
Down to the town square
We'd put on free shows
No one could see there
We'd do our two step
Behind a thicket
And for applause, Matt
We had a cricket
We had a cricket
A cricket's fine and so's a son
To fill the evening's empty air
A cricket's not Ed Sullivan
Or satin gowns or fancy hair
And Idaho is not Detroit
Not if you're young, not if you're black
It's just a place you should avoid
Stay on your jet and don't look back

Where did my dreams go
Where did my life go
I have no answers
I have a son, though
Without his father

I don't have that
Without a husband
But I have Matt

You'll pass our dreams on
You'll keep them going
You're such a sweet boy
And how you're growing

You won't be lonely
Won't have to play act
To keep from crying
Get out of Mosco
You'll fight your way out
And you'll keep trying
And you'll keep trying
Goodbye, Matt
Life is a lie, Matt
I hardly knew it
You helped me through it
And now you're gone, Matt

And now you're gone—Mom
And now you're gone, Mom

And only Matt goes on
And only Matt goes on

(Lights dim on MATT. *After a while an eerie dim light gradually comes up as* LUKE *enters in a disheveled state, looking for his shirt,* MATT *is in shadow at first unseen by* LUKE.*)*

LUKE: Matt?

(No response from MATT*)*

LUKE: Hey. You sleep walkin'? What's a matter?

(Still no response)

LUKE: Matt? C'mon buddy, you're scarin' me. What's a matter? How long you been awake?

MATT: A long time.

LUKE: You wanna come lie by me a while. I'll help you sleep.

MATT: That's what my mother used to say to me.

LUKE: What?

MATT: She would lay on my bed and tell me I was all she had and she would sing to me and…touch… 'Til I was twelve and big as she was and said "Momma, you gotta stop it, you can't do that anymore. Go back to your own bed."

LUKE: Oh god, Matt.

MATT: I don't think she knew what she was doing. We so seldom do. I ought to be leaving you.

LUKE: Please, Matt, please. Don't go. Stay and talk to me. You can tell me anything. Please. Anything. Tell me—

MATT: Suppose you tell me…what happened tonight?

LUKE: I think I did a bad thing, Matt.

MATT: Why?

LUKE: Because I was confused. He just ignores me. When I ask him why we're here he just fucks with me. Does he think that question is just gonna go away? I didn't know how else to get through to him. And I was so crazy for someone to touch me. But now I feel worse than before. Please come lay beside me. Just let me hold you for a little while. So I can sleep. Tell my why we're here. Tell me we're alive or dead. Tell me something I can hold onto.

MATT: Please don't ask me to do that.

LUKE: You're not mad because I did it with Jon, are you? You know I'd rather be with you. Sometimes when he would touch me I'd pretend it was you. But you pushed me away, Matt. Right? You pushed me away. You're still my buddy, huh? Matt? Please, don't push me away again.

MATT: Why didn't you stay with him?

LUKE: He wanted me to. He begged me. But I couldn't. I wanted to hurt him. Make him need me. And he did. He really begged.

MATT: Did he?

LUKE: But I only want to be with you. You don't make me feel alone like he does. You listen to me. You see me.

MATT: Oh.

LUKE: What'sa matter? I didn't hurt you, did I? Matt, how? You pushed me away. You didn't want me. All you had to do…oh, no…

(realizing the truth)

You and Jon? Oh, Matt, I'm sorry…I would never do anything to hurt you…I mean if I'd known I would never…Matt, please be my buddy—please—stay my friend…

(MATT turns his back on LUKE, LUKE falls to his knees)

MATT: *(After a beat)* Ssshh. Sssshh.

(MATT moves over to LUKE and rocks him)

Lullaby

You're in an empty space
You watch life come your way
The darkness bears his face
And you know why you stay
You feel your future race
And then it's held at bay

And you're left aching
'Rina, close your eyes

It's just your heart that's breaking
Don't give up on kindness
Save yourself a lashing
Love is always timeless
Sorrow's only passing

You're on an empty stage
Tomorrow comes your way
You turn an empty page
There are no word to say
In Moscow

(Lights slowly dim, then hold on this new world Pieta.
MATT *lays* LUKE's *head gently on* LUKE's *arm with perhaps*
some curtain or LUKE's *sweatshirt as a pillow.* MATT *exits.*
LUKE's *eyes flash open. He feels himself to be truly alone. He*
sees some of the rope that hangs about the stage in disarray.
He mounts one of the open ladders on the stage, grabs a
hanging rope, tugs at it to test its hold and wraps it around
his neck. JON *enters through the audience.)*

JON: *(Joking)* What the hell are you doing up there?
Oh my god was I that bad tonight? I know it's been a
while, but... *(Realizing then, slowly:)* Luke? Luke, what
are you doing?

LUKE: Please. Go away.

JON: What are you doing?

LUKE: I can't go on like this. I have to know. Are we
alive or dead? I can't stand it anymore. Go away. *Get*
out of here.

Listen, Luke

JON: Stay where you are, Luke.

LUKE: Don't come near me.

JON: *(Approaching* LUKE *gently)*
You want some answers
I want some too

LUKE: I have to know, Jon
I have to know
Get off the ladder
Or I'll let go

JON: What would be different if you knew
The truth

How would it change the way you feel
For me
For Matt
For you
You think that suddenly there'll be a reason
For why we do
The things we do

JON:	LUKE:
What if there's no reason	There has to be a reason
What if there's no meaning	I won't pretend, Jon
The world out there is gone,	Not to see what you
Luke	won't see
It isn't worth retrieving	
There's only here, Luke	
There's only now	
I don't know why, Luke	
I don't know how	
The earth was round, Luke	
And now it's flat	
There's only you, Luke	
And me and Matt	
There's no above, son	
There's no below	
I'm climbing up, Luke	
Please don't let go	
Slip off the rope, Luke	
Please don't let go	
It's not all black, Luke	
It's not all white	
It's not all wrong, son	

It's not all right
But it's okay, Luke
But it's okay

(LUKE *has gone passive and let* JON *remove the rope*)

LUKE: Why didn't you let me go? You had no right to stop me. I should have jumped and taken you with me. With your weight and mine for sure my neck would crack. Then maybe we'd know. Or at least I'd be past caring.

JON: Luke—

LUKE: You're always trying to stop me. Shutting me up. You can't deal with my questions. So you make fun of me for even asking.

JON: For godsake, Luke, you were trying to kill yourself.

LUKE: So you're sure then. We are alive.

JON: I don't know. I just try to hold on. Keep my eyes on us. On what we can do here. What we can make of this. *(Pause)* I thought that… maybe after tonight… you'd have a little more to hold on to. You left so quickly—

LUKE: That's what you thought? You always think you have all the fucking answers, don't you? *Tonight?!*

JON: Why did you run away?

LUKE: You don't even know what happened tonight. I fucked everything up. I never should have touched you. I wish to God I'd never touched you.

Listen, Luke *(continued)*

JON: Listen, Luke
I'm grateful that you touched me
Wanted so to touch you
I wanted to excite you

Feel myself inside you
I trembled so inside you
You did not do anything wrong
It's okay
Watching from above you
Thinking I could love you
Don't be sorry that it happened
Shall I say I'm sorry
Lie and say that I'm sorry too

LUKE: Jon, don't be so stupid
You don't know what I'm saying
I wanted to hurt you
Knock you off your high horse
(Forcing JON *off the ladder)*
Wanted to abuse you
Wanted to control you
Wanted to reduce you

Just to see how low
You could get
You fell a little more
Than I'd bet

JON: And now you're feeling guilty,
Contrite
No need to be concerned
I'm alright

LUKE:
(Coming off the ladder, lacerating JON *with the words)*
This is not about you
I don't give a fuck about you
You're nothing but a phoney
This is about Matthew
What I've done to Matthew
Do you know that he loves you
How could somebody love you
It never even entered my mind

I never would have been that unkind
Oh god he must be lonely right now

JON: I thought I could control it
Put it all behind me
Until you stole behind me

LUKE: How can you tell me
This is not hell
If we had a window
We could watch the burning
If we had a mirror
We could see the devil
My father always told me
A mirror is a window
To hell
The edges have a bevel
And there you see the devil
In shame

There you see the devil
He said
If this is life I'd rather
Be dead
I wish we had a window,
Don't you
A high and open window
A hold that I could crawl through
A window I could fall through
To flame

(MATT *has entered and places the broken broom handle on
the floor in front of* LUKE *which they use to denote a window
when they perform* Three Sisters, *and gestures to* LUKE *that
indeed they do have a window:)*

MATT: Look out the window
The fire is flaring
It must be a silo
And all that dry wheat

The night's getting colder
In spite of the heat
I feel ten years older—

LUKE: *(Trying for the first time to grasp it)*
I—I—I can't remember
The Italian for window
(To MATT*)*
Help me.

Italian For Window

MATT/MASHA: I can't remember that song mother sang

LUKE/IRINA: And everyday I forget something more
Sitting at the council

MATT/MASHA: Sitting in the bedroom

LUKE/IRINA: Wasting in the townhall

MATT/MASHA: Looking out my window

LUKE/IRINA: Growing old and bitter

MATT/MASHA: Something about summer

LUKE/IRINA: Moaning like a quitter

MATT/MASHA: Beaches on the Black Sea

LUKE/IRINA: Someone ought to twit me

MATT/MASHA: Peaches on a fig tree

LUKE/IRINA: Bring me to my senses

MATT/MASHA: Help me to remember

LUKE/IRINA: What was that conjunction

MATT/MASHA: Olya, how'd that song go

LUKE/IRINA: Now I've lost the tenses

MATT/MASHA: Fading like an ember

LUKE/IRINA: Everything is slipping

MATT/MASHA: Everything is fading

LUKE/IRINA: Away

MATT/MASHA: Something else with each passing day

LUKE/IRINA: Something else we'll never get back

MATT/MASHA: A shiny coin that slips through a crack

LUKE/IRINA: I'll never have a husband
All my life I thought
He'd be there
Awaiting me in Moscow's
Great square
(Reaching for MATT*)*
Onyx eyes and black
Wavy hair

MATT/MASHA: Can you remember
At the Baron's arrival
How much we giggled
How funny he seemed
Dressed for a revival
His speech slightly salival
His Russian was archival

Now see how we love him
You know you respect him
Baron has a good heart
And head
Long nights won't be barren
In bed
See if our sister will
Give her approval
Could I remarry
That's what I'd do
Such a kind proposal
He's at your disposal
No guarantee your woes will
Abate
But marry him before it's
Too late

(Gesturing to JON*)*
The Baron is a window
Open up the window
Go through
Maybe you'll find peace if
You do
Peace and something extra
Dear as a medallion
Olya, why so silent
Surely you approve
Surely you approve

JON/OLGA: *(To avoid, to change the subject)*
Sisters, its finestra
A window in Italian

MATT/MASHA: Of course we should have known it
If you have a question
If you have a problem

Headmistress has the answer
She's the one to solve it
Well, here's another problem

(Growing increasingly unrelenting, letting all his pent up feelings finally come out onto JON *as the three men merge with their* Three Sisters *personae sweeping them toward the climax)*

MATT/MASHA:
Olga, forgive me
For this indiscretion
But I can't keep silent
I have a confession
My soul has a longing
That I can't assuage or
Deny—I'm in love with
Out own love-sick major

JON/OLGA: You don't know what you're saying

MATT/MASHA: Olya, you must hear me
I know that you don't want to

JON/OLGA: Stop this or I'm going

MATT/MASHA: Olya, please stay near me
It's something I can't undo
I love everything about him

JON/OLGA: *(With his hands over his ears, singing to block out* MATT/MASHA*)*
Peaches in the Black Sea

MATT/MASHA: You'd have me live without him

JON/OLGA: Breezes in a fig tree

MATT/MASHA: Olya, don't ignore me

JON/OLGA: Beaches in the country

MATT/MASHA: I love his fire, his sad grin
His wry philosophizing

JON/OLGA: The very things about him
You ought to be despising

MATT/MASHA: When one reads a fiction
It all seems formulaic
But life's a strange addiction
And never that prosaic

JON/OLGA: It has to be it's platonic

MATT/MASHA: And if it's not, forgive me
Does that make me demonic
Surely not comparatively
(Gesturing to his two compatriots)
You know it is ironic
Though you reproach me, blame me
Beneath the moral tonic
We really are the same three
We walk the same low country
Wishing we could change our past
Wond'ring how we'll live our lives

If we knew we'd be aghast
Wait, tomorrow soon arrives.

LUKE: I think
Tomorrow has arrived.

LUKE & MATT: *(Together, to* JON*)*
We'll never get to Moscow
How could we believe
That we would
Moscow is a dream
Gone for good

We'll never get to Moscow
Of all the wishes God
Could endow
We wanted one that He
Won't allow
We'll never get to
Never
Get to
Moscow

(After the crescendo and resolve of this last duet between
LUKE *and* MATT, *there is silence. Finally* JON *begins*
quietly:)

JON: I thought I could teach you
To survive in here
Thought that I could help you
Find a window

But I can't keep my own dead
Dreams alive in here
How dare I think that I
Had found an answer

I only found a way to
Hide the question

What are we?

LUKE: Three ghosts.

JON: Is that true?

MATT: We hear what we need to hear
See what we need to see
Are who we need to be
'Til life pulls back a curtain
Then maybe some truth is revealed

Though maybe nothing certain
Maybe just another curtain
Hiding less than the last one concealed

It's time.

JON: I can't.

MATT: You can. I'll help you.

Chekhov's Finale

MATT: You hear a band play
Strings and flutes, an oboe
Me, I hear gay martial music fading
It lures a lovesick major with its fife
Beguiles him with its melody
And carries him away from me
To take him to his daughters and his wife
(Trying one more time to bring JON *in)*
You hear a band play
Strings and flute—

JON: *(Broken, he joins reluctantly)*
An oboe—
We are left alone to start anew here
Don't know if that is something I can do
Beguiled by the illusory
Delusions are what carried me
Now I can't believe I'll ever muddle through

LUKE: *(As* MATT *beckons him back into the play)*
I only hear a solo
On a lonely horn

I kneel to pray
But cannot mourn

(To JON, *placing* JON's *hands upon* JON's *chest, to make peace, to let* JON *know* LUKE *understands what* JON *has been trying to do.* LUKE *is singing about their lives:)*

LUKE: A man I didn't love
Has died today
Died in a duel
How passé
A duel
I want to think he died a fool
But at least he died for something
Even though it was for nothing
He thought it was for something
That is something, isn't it?
At least I think so
I am spared my empty vow
God has intervened somehow
(Offering this talk of God to JON *as a suggestion of what might be happening to them)*
And He involves Himself so seldom now

MATT, LUKE, JON: *(Together:)*
If we looked back
Eleven years ago
Back when we got here
All we would see were dreams
And baseless yearning

We knew by now we'd be in Moscow
We knew for sure our lives would flower
We'd ride the broad streets in a landau
And field our suitors by the hour
So sweet to yearn, yet no discerning
So much to learn, but not much learning

LUKE: A time will come with we will know
Why there is misery

They'll be no mysteries, you'll see
(Looking through the fourth wall and really seeing)

Look at the trees
The leaves are turning

JON: Burning

MATT: Brightening

LUKE: They'll soon have fallen

JON: I love Autumn
But it's frightening

MATT: Look in the east
The sky is raging

JON: Slaking

LUKE: Changing

MATT: Oh there's a firefly

LUKE: In the twilight
Stars are waking

MATT: The music is so joyful

LUKE: So tender

JON: So mournful

MATT: *(To get* JON *to see, to pull* JON *in)*
So splendid
No more dour recrimination
While we hear such jubilation

LUKE: *(Pointing out through the fourth wall)*
See the sky's illumination

JON: *(Still reluctant, hanging back a bit)*
In the distance

MATT: Life is insistent

LUKE: We are proceeding

JON: *(Finally stepping into it, as* MATT *and* LUKE *welcome him)*
We are resistant

MATT, LUKE, JON:
Sisters are resilient
The sunset is so brilliant

MATT: Forget the future
Forget the past
Only this moment

MATT, LUKE, JON:
Only we sisters
Will last.

END OF PLAY

www.ingramcontent.com/pod-product-compliance
Lightning Source LLC
Chambersburg PA
CBHW070024110426
42741CB00034B/2529